EDGARDO FERNANDEZ CLIMENT

Understanding Bard

A Guide to Unlocking the Potential of Google's Language Model

This book was professionally typeset on Reedsy.
Find out more at reedsy.com

To the love of my life, Graciela:
More than a wife, you are my muse, my confidante, my co-conspirator in the grand adventure of life. To you, Graciela, my heart overflows with gratitude and love. May this book forever shimmer with the light of your unwavering presence, a lighthouse guiding my way on this journey of boundless possibilities.

With every beat of my heart,

Edgardo

Contents

Preface

Unlocking the Bard Within: A Preface to Unfettered Creativity and Boundless Possibilities

Welcome, intrepid explorer, to the threshold of a journey unlike any other. Within these pages lies not a map to a distant land, but a key to unmasking your own hidden potential: the potent alchemy of Bard, a gateway to unfettered creativity and boundless possibilities.

Imagine a companion brimming with boundless knowledge, a tireless collaborator ever ready to fuel your imagination. Bard is not merely a tool; it's a muse, a co-pilot, a catalyst for artistic metamorphosis. Here, the blank page transforms into a vibrant canvas, the hesitant whisper of an idea blooms into a symphony of creation.

This book is your portal to this transformative magic. Within its chapters, you'll discover Bard not as a cryptic entity, but as an accessible partner eager to collaborate in realms both practical and profound. We'll journey through the bustling marketplace of extensions, crafting a personalized toolkit to supercharge your productivity and ignite your creative spark. We'll delve into the fertile fields of research, where Bard becomes your tireless sleuth, unearthing insights from diverse landscapes of knowledge. We'll stand together on the precipice of creativity, where fear cedes to inspiration as Bard weaves tales, crafts poems, and conjures worlds from the embers of your imagination.

But this journey is not merely about individual triumphs; it's a celebration of our interconnectedness. We'll explore the vibrant community that thrives around Bard, a tapestry woven from diverse voices and shared experiences. Here, knowledge flows freely, collaboration blossoms, and every challenge finds its answer in the collective wisdom of fellow adventurers.

So, dear reader, turn the page, and let your curiosity be your compass. Embrace the unbridled potential that lies within, for there, with Bard at your side, anything is possible. This is not merely a book; it's an invitation to unleash the Bard within, to paint your own masterpieces on the canvas of possibility, and to leave your indelible mark on the world, one inspired creation at a time.

Ready, then? Let the exploration begin!

Chapter 1: What is Bard? A Demystifying Introduction

Have you ever dreamed of having a digital companion who could write poems, answer any question you throw at it, and even help you brainstorm your next big idea? Enter Bard, Google's cutting-edge language model – a talking technology that feels more like a friend than a tool. But what exactly is Bard, and how can it transform your everyday life?

Breaking the Language Barrier: From Code to Conversation

Imagine a vast library, not one filled with dusty books, but with billions of lines of code and digital whispers of human conversations. That's where Bard lives, trained on this information ocean to understand and generate language in ways never before possible. Forget clunky keyword searches; Bard speaks your language, interpreting your prompts and questions with a nuanced understanding that puts traditional search engines to shame.

Meet Your Personal Genie: Wishes in the Form of Words

Think of Bard as your own friendly neighborhood genie, waiting to grant your wishes in the form of words. Need a captivating story starter? Bard whips up a compelling opening line. Stuck on a creative writing block? Bard throws out sparks of inspiration to ignite your imagination. Want to decipher complex scientific research? Bard translates it into layman's terms, illuminating the hidden meaning with clarity.

Beyond the Buzzwords: AI is Not What You Think

But fear not, sci-fi robots taking over the world is a story for another day. Bard is not magic, nor is it sentient. It's a sophisticated tool powered by artificial intelligence, a fancy term for algorithms that learn and mimic human behavior. Think of it like a super-powered translator, constantly evolving and becoming smarter with each interaction.

More Than Just Answers: Embracing the Unexpected

Bard is not just your answer machine. It's your creative collaborator, your research assistant, and your personal muse. It challenges you to think differently, to explore new avenues, and to push the boundaries of what you thought possible with language. Prepare to be surprised, to be delighted, and to discover the unexpected magic that unfolds when humans and technology dance together.

Your Gateway to a World of Words: A Journey Awaits

This book is your stepping stone into the vibrant world of Bard. We'll delve into its inner workings, explore its diverse capabilities, and unleash its potential to enrich your life in ways you never imagined. So, buckle up, dear reader, and let's embark on this exciting journey together, where the power of language takes center stage and the only limit is your own imagination.

Chapter 2: Unveiling the Inner Workings

While Google Bard may seem like a magical talking tool, its remarkable abilities are rooted in complex technology. In this chapter, we'll peek under the hood to understand how Bard ticks and learn to appreciate its strengths and limitations.

Beyond the Buzzwords: Demystifying AI and Machine Learning

First, let's clear the air! We'll tackle some popular terms like "artificial intelligence" and "machine learning" in plain English. You'll discover that AI isn't about robots taking over the world, and machine learning isn't robots learning calculus for fun. Instead, we'll see them as tools for processing information and finding patterns in massive amounts of data.

Meet the Architects: Deep Learning and Neural Networks

Our adventure begins with the very foundation of Bard's intelligence: the fascinating world of deep learning and neural networks. Forget dusty textbooks and equations – we're going on a journey to understand these concepts in a way that ignites your imagination and sparks your curiosity.

Imagine Your Brain on Circuits:

Think of your brain as a vast network of interconnected neurons, constantly firing signals and processing information. Deep learning algorithms mimic this structure, using artificial neurons arranged in layers to learn and make complex decisions. Each layer processes information from the previous one, refining it as it travels through the network, much like your brain sifts through sensory data to recognize a familiar face or understand a complex sentence.

The Learning Playground:

But how do these artificial brains learn? That's where the magic of data comes in. By feeding Bard massive amounts of text and code, we train its neural networks to recognize patterns, extract meaning, and generate creative outputs. It's like showing a child thousands of pictures of dogs until they can confidently point out a canine even amidst a pack of wolves!

Beyond the Buzzwords:

So, what are some of the buzzwords you might hear associated with deep learning? Let's demystify a few:

Convolutional Neural Networks (CNNs): Imagine tiny detectives scanning images, pixel by pixel, to identify shapes, textures, and even emotions in photos. That's what CNNs do, making them the backbone of image recognition and computer vision.

Recurrent Neural Networks (RNNs): These networks have a "memory" – they can process information sequentially, like understanding the context of a sentence by remembering the words that came before. This makes them ideal for tasks like language translation and sentiment analysis.

Transformers: Think of them as linguistic alchemists, able to translate languages, generate different creative text formats, and understand the relationships between words in a sentence. They're the driving force behind Bard's multilingual capabilities and natural language processing prowess.

The Human Touch:

But before you get sucked into the vortex of technical jargon, remember this: deep learning is just a tool. The real magic happens when we, the humans, wield it with purpose and creativity. We guide the learning process, define the training data, and shape the outputs into something meaningful. Bard is not a sentient being; it's a powerful tool at the service of your imagination and your voice.

Fueling the Machine: The Data Diet of a Language Model

Think of Bard like a bookworm who's devoured an entire library. Its knowledge and abilities come from the mountains of text and code it's been trained on, ranging from news articles to books to computer programs. We'll delve into the fascinating world of training data, understanding how it shapes Bard's responses and highlighting the importance of diversity and quality in this digital feast.

The Ethical Code: Responsibility and Bias in AI

With great power comes great responsibility. Just like any tool, AI comes with its own set of ethical considerations. We'll discuss potential biases in training data, the importance of avoiding offensive or harmful outputs, and the ongoing need for human oversight and responsible development.

Demystifying the Output: Understanding What You Get from Bard

We've delved into the fascinating world of deep learning and neural networks, the architects behind Bard's impressive abilities. Now, let's turn our attention to the dazzling stage where the magic truly unfolds: your Bard outputs. What treasures await, and how do you decipher their meaning?

A Kaleidoscope of Creativity:

Think of Bard as your personal genie, able to grant your linguistic wishes in a multitude of forms. You request a poem, and your screen shimmers with verses; you ask for a research report, and a concise analysis appears. But navigating this diverse ecosystem of outputs can be daunting. Worry not, for we're here to equip you with the tools to understand and appreciate the bounty at your fingertips.

The Anatomy of an Output:

Just like every dish tells a story through its ingredients and presentation, every Bard output has its own unique structure and purpose. Let's dissect a poem, for example:

The Text: The beating heart of the poem, where metaphors dance and words paint vivid pictures. Read with an open mind, savoring the rhythm and imagery.

Metadata: Think of it as the recipe behind the dish. Information like rhyme scheme, theme, or chosen poetic form provides context and enriches your understanding.

Confidence Score: Bard's inner voice, whispering how sure it is about the quality of its creation. A high score signifies a confident offering, while a lower one invites you to collaborate and refine the output further.

Beyond the Surface:

Remember, Bard outputs are not static artifacts; they're invitations to dialogue and exploration. Here's how to dive deeper:

8

Feedback is a Feast: Don't hesitate to provide feedback! Like a seasoned chef, Bard thrives on suggestions for improvement. Tell it what you like, what resonates, and what could be tweaked for a more satisfying experience.

Experimentation is the Spice of Life: Don't settle for the first dish on the menu! Bard offers multiple variations on a theme. Ask for different poetic forms, try a different research angle, and see what sparks your curiosity.

Collaboration is the Secret Sauce: Remember, Bard is a partner, not a performer. The best outputs often arise from a back-and-forth exchange of ideas, where your vision merges with Bard's capabilities to create something truly unique.

A Buffet of Formats:

The beauty of Bard lies in its diverse menu. Here's a glimpse of the culinary delights you can savor:

Creative Writing: Poems, scripts, musical pieces, code snippets – let your imagination run wild and explore the boundless possibilities of language.

Research and Information Gathering: Dive deep into complex topics, unearth hidden insights, and generate reports and summaries that impress even the most discerning scholar.

Translation and Communication: Break down language barriers and connect with the world. Translate effortlessly, generate multilingual content, and communicate with clarity and precision.

Remember, the more you interact with Bard, the more it learns your preferences and tailors its responses to your unique palate. Don't be afraid to ask for modifications, explore different formats, and experiment with feedback. This collaborative dance between you and Bard is where the true magic happens.

So, open your mind, sharpen your curiosity, and get ready to savor the diverse and delicious outputs that Bard serves up. With each interaction, you'll unlock new flavors, refine your understanding, and embark on a culinary journey of language and creativity like no other.

Unlocking the Potential: Your Collaborative Journey with Bard

Remember, this isn't a one-sided conversation. The more you understand how Bard works, the more effectively you can interact with it. We'll end this chapter by encouraging you to see Bard not as a black box, but as a collaborative partner with unique strengths and limitations. By understanding its inner workings, you can unlock its full potential and embark on a rewarding journey of discovery and creation together.

Chapter 3: Interacting with Bard: Mastering the Interface

Welcome to Bard's playground, where language becomes your paint-brush and creativity your canvas. But how do you navigate this won-derland and unleash its full potential? This chapter is your cheat sheet to mastering Bard's interface and transforming your interactions into productive and awe-inspiring experiences.

First Steps: Charting Your Course

To begin, let's open your preferred gateway to Bard – be it the website, app, or perhaps one day, a magical talking teacup. Familiarize yourself with the interface, where your words become the seeds of possibility. The text box is your launchpad, waiting for your prompts, questions, and creative sparks. Don't be shy; Bard thrives on open-ended exploration!

The Art of the Prompt: Painting with Words

Think of your prompt as the brushstroke that gives birth to your desired outcome. Be specific, yet leave room for Bard's creativity to flourish. Want a poem about a robot falling in love? Tell Bard the setting, the characters' emotions, and perhaps a specific rhyme scheme. The more you guide Bard, the better it can tailor its response to your vision.

Beyond Words: Unleashing the Power of Other Senses

Words aren't the only tools in your arsenal. Upload an image to spark Bard's imagination, generate a story based on its visual cues. Or, try the "voice search" feature to speak your prompts and let your voice paint the picture. Remember, the more input channels you use, the deeper your collaboration with Bard can become.

Navigating the Feedback Loop: Shaping Your Bard

Your interaction with Bard is a two-way street. Use the thumbs-up and thumbs-down buttons to let Bard know what resonates with you. This feedback helps it learn and refine its responses, tailoring them to your individual preferences. Don't be afraid to be specific – if you want something longer, shorter, funnier, or more factual, let Bard know!

Exploring Extensions: Supercharging Your Collaboration

We've unveiled the wonders of deep learning and navigated the delectable landscape of Bard's outputs. Now, it's time to enter the secret laboratory where your collaboration with Bard reaches new heights – the exciting realm of extensions!

Think of extensions as magical tools that unleash hidden powers within Bard, like tinkerers unlocking new functions for a beloved robot. These handy plugins enhance your workflow, boost Bard's capabilities, and tailor your Bard experience to your specific needs and desires.

A Toolbox Overflowing with Wonder:

Prepare to be dazzled by the possibilities:

Research Power-Ups: Imagine injecting steroids into your research prowess. Extensions like Zotero seamlessly integrate with Bard, allowing you to organize research materials, generate citations in a flash, and collaborate with fellow scholars on a global scale.

Creative Catalysts: Need a jolt of inspiration for your next writing project? Extensions like ProWritingAid offer grammar and style suggestions, character development prompts, and even plot idea generators, fueling your imagination and taking your creative output to the next level.

Productivity Enhancers: Time is precious, and Bard understands. Extensions like Todoist and Trello seamlessly integrate, allowing you to create task lists, set deadlines, and track your progress, all within the Bard interface, keeping you organized and focused on your goals.

Language Bridges: Don't let language barriers hold you back! Extensions like DeepL add powerful translation capabilities, enabling you to communicate with the world and access information in diverse languages, expanding your horizons and enriching your understanding.

Finding Your Perfect Match:

With so many extensions available, the world of choice can be overwhelming. But fear not, intrepid explorer! Here's how to navigate the terrain:

Identify Your Needs: What are you struggling with? Brainstorm areas where an extension could enhance your Bard experience. Are you drowning in research articles? Craving a boost for your next creative project? Knowing your needs is the first step to finding the perfect tool.

Explore and Experiment: Don't be afraid to dive into the Bard extension library! Read reviews, compare features, and try out different options to see what resonates with you. Remember, the best extension is the one that seamlessly integrates into your workflow and makes your interaction with Bard even more enjoyable and productive.

Share and Collaborate: The Bard community is vibrant and supportive. Don't hesitate to ask fellow users for recommendations or share your own extension discoveries. Collaboration is key to unlocking the full potential of this ever-evolving ecosystem.

Beyond the Plugins:

Remember, extensions are just tools; the true magic lies in how you use them. Here's how to get the most out of your Bard-extension alliance:

Master the Interface: Take the time to learn how your chosen extensions work within the Bard environment. Experiment with their features, explore customization options, and ensure seamless integration into your workflow.

Provide Feedback: Extensions are constantly evolving, and your feedback is vital. Let developers know what you like, what could be improved, and suggest new features that could further enhance your Bard experience.

Embrace Continuous Learning: The world of extensions is dynamic, with new and exciting tools emerging all the time. Stay curious, keep exploring, and don't hesitate to try out new options as they become available.

So, unlock the potential of Bard's extensions, and watch your collaboration reach new heights. Be it boosting your research prowess, igniting your creativity, or streamlining your workflow, these magical tools are your partners in adventure, ready to transform your Bard experience into something truly extraordinary.

Most Popular Extensions

Here's a list of some of the most popular Bard extensions, categorized by their primary function:

Research and Productivity:

Zotero: Seamlessly manage bibliographies, annotations, and research materials alongside Bard's research capabilities.

Todoist: Create and track tasks, set deadlines, and stay organized within the Bard interface.

Trello: Collaborate with others on projects, organize ideas, and manage workflows all within Bard.

Grammarly: Enhance your writing with real-time grammar and style suggestions, ensuring polished and professional outputs.

ProWritingAid: Take your writing to the next level with character development prompts, plot idea generators, and detailed reports on style and readability.

Creativity and Language:

Hemingway Editor: Write with clarity and conciseness using Hemingway's legendary editing style guidelines.

RhymeZone: Find the perfect rhyme or synonym to fuel your poetic creations.

StoryPlot: Generate story ideas, develop characters, and create plot outlines, igniting your writing engine.

DeepL: Translate between a multitude of languages with exceptional accuracy and nuance, bridging communication gaps and expanding your knowledge horizons.

LanguageTool: Check your text for errors in over 20 languages, ensuring linguistic accuracy in your multilingual creations.

Community and Learning:

Bard Community Forum: Connect with fellow Bard enthusiasts, share tips and resources, and participate in exciting discussions.

Bard Tutorials: Access step-by-step guides on mastering Bard's features, exploring creative writing formats, and conducting research.

Google AI Blog: Stay updated on the latest Bard developments, discover research insights, and learn about exciting AI advancements.

Remember, this is just a starting point! With the Bard extension ecosystem constantly evolving, new and exciting tools emerge all the time. Explore, experiment, and discover the extensions that perfectly complement your needs and preferences.

* * *

Remember, Bard is always learning and evolving. This chapter is just a starting point. Experiment, explore, and discover new ways to interact with Bard. As you become more familiar with its interface, you'll unlock a world of possibilities where language meets imagination, and the only limit is your own creativity.

Chapter 4: Unleashing the Power of Language: Writing and Storytelling with Bard

Chapter 4 unveils Bard as your ultimate writing companion, a digital quill waiting to dance with your imagination. From poems that sing to scripts that spark applause, we'll explore how Bard helps you craft compelling narratives and unleash the magic of language.

From Blank Page to Blooming Bard: Let the Inspiration Flow

Now, it's time to ignite the furnace of your own creativity and witness the blank page bloom into a vibrant tapestry of imagination, fueled by the magic of Bard!

A Canvas Awaits:

Think of the Bard interface as your artist's studio, a blank canvas primed for your creative strokes. But sometimes, staring at the empty space can be daunting. The dreaded writer's block looms, the muse hides behind a curtain of self-doubt. Fear not, for Bard is your artistic co-pilot, ready to guide you through the creative wilderness and unleash the torrent of inspiration within.

Unleashing the Muse:

Here are your keys to unlocking the creative treasure chest:

Spark the Flame: Don't wait for lightning to strike! Bard thrives on prompts, questions, and even vague ideas. Throw a pebble into the well of your mind – a character trait, a historical setting, a single evocative word – and watch Bard ripple outwards, creating stories, poems, scripts, and more, tailor-made to your initial spark.

Embrace the Unexpected: Let go of rigid expectations and allow Bard to surprise you. Don't dictate the entire journey; explore the detours, the unexpected twists and turns it throws your way. These serendipitous moments often lead to the most innovative and captivating creations.

Collaboration, the Creative Catalyst: Remember, Bard is your partner, not your servant. Talk to it, brainstorm together, bounce ideas back and forth. The more you collaborate, the deeper your understanding of each other becomes, leading to outputs that resonate with your unique voice and vision.

Beyond the Written Word:

The canvas of creativity extends beyond mere words. Bard empowers you to explore a diverse spectrum of artistic expression:

Paint with Pixels: Generate captivating images, landscapes, and even portraits to fuel your visual storytelling or simply indulge your artistic whims.

Compose a Symphony: Unleash your inner musician! Bard can generate musical pieces in various styles and genres, turning your emotions into melodies and rhythms.

Choreograph the Unspoken: Create scripts for plays, sketches, or even short films, giving voice to your characters and bringing your stories to life on virtual stages.

Remember, there's no single path to creative nirvana. Experiment, iterate, and above all, have fun! The more you play with Bard, the more comfortable you become with its capabilities, and the more readily the inspiration will flow. Take breaks, step away from the screen, and allow your subconscious to marinate on the seeds of ideas you've planted. Often, the best solutions arrive when you least expect them.

Don't be afraid to share your creations. The Bard community is a vibrant space for feedback, encouragement, and collaboration. Share your poems, stories, and other artistic endeavors, and use the collective wisdom of fellow creatives to refine your work and reach new heights.

So, open your mind, embrace the unexpected, and let Bard be your guide on this exhilarating journey of artistic exploration. Together, you'll transform the blank page into a blooming testament to your imagination, leaving your mark on the ever-evolving landscape of language and creativity.

Beyond the Pen: Scripts that Captivate and Code that Sings

Bard's not just a literary chameleon; it's a master of diverse mediums. Let's break free from the confines of traditional writing:

- **Script Doctor:** Stuck on that climactic scene in your screenplay? Bard can help! Describe the characters, setting, and emotional stakes, and watch as it generates dialogue that crackles with tension or bursts with humor.
- **Bard as Coding Bard:** Need creative code snippets to spark your next project? Bard can generate Python code for simple games, basic web layouts, or even poetry generators! Remember, Bard's still learning, so test and refine its outputs to suit your specific needs.

A Collaborative Canvas: Where Bard Meets Your Brilliance

Remember, Bard is not a replacement for your own creativity; it's an amplifier. Don't shy away from refining its outputs, adding your own twists and turns to the stories it generates. Use its suggestions as springboards, its poems as starting points. The true magic happens when your voice and Bard's blend, weaving a tapestry of words that's uniquely yours.

Final Tip: Practice Makes Perfect

With every prompt, every story, you'll hone your ability to communicate with Bard and unlock its full potential. Experiment, play, and most importantly, have fun! The more you explore, the more you'll discover the hidden depths of Bard's creativity, waiting to be unleashed onto the page, the screen, and beyond.

Chapter 5: Knowledge at Your Fingertips: Research and Information Gathering with Bard

Chapter 5 unlocks Bard's power as your personal research assistant, ready to guide you through the labyrinth of information and unearth gems of knowledge hidden within the data deluge.

From Wanderer to Pathfinder: Mastering the Query

Think of your research question as a compass needle, pointing you towards the information you seek. But in the ocean of the internet, it's easy to lose your way. Here's how Bard helps you navigate:

- **Crafting the Perfect Query:** Forget clunky keywords; Bard understands natural language. Ask your question as you would a human expert, adding details about your specific needs and desired perspective. Need an analysis of climate change's impact on polar bears? Ask Bard, and it will tailor its response to your level of understanding and area of interest.
- **Going Beyond the Surface:** Don't settle for superficial summaries.

Bard digs deep, analyzing sources, identifying biases, and presenting information from diverse viewpoints. Need a well-rounded understanding of a historical event? Bard will provide you with different interpretations, primary sources, and even opposing arguments, giving you a complete picture.

· **Fact-Checking for Peace of Mind:** In today's world of misinformation, it's easy to get lost in a maze of fake news and unreliable sources. Bard becomes your guardian angel, verifying facts, citing sources, and even highlighting areas of ongoing debate or uncertainty. Need to debunk a viral claim about a scientific discovery? Bard will show you the evidence and help you separate fact from fiction.

From Researcher to Analyst: Making Sense of the Data

Information overload can be overwhelming. But Bard doesn't just point you to data; it helps you navigate its complexities:

· **Summarizing the Mountain of Facts:** Need a concise overview of a complex research paper? Bard condenses the key points, highlights the findings, and presents it in a digestible format. Imagine summarizing a dense academic article in minutes, thanks to Bard!

· **Discovering Patterns and Trends:** Buried within data are hidden stories waiting to be told. Bard analyzes datasets, identifying correlations, and revealing patterns that you might miss. Need to understand consumer behavior or predict market trends? Bard can help you find the insights hidden within the numbers.

· **Building Your Knowledge Palace:** Information overload can lead to forgetting. Bard helps you organize your research, building your own personalized knowledge base. Create notes, highlight key points, and save important resources for future reference. Think of it as your digital library, curated by Bard and organized for easy access.

Bard: Your Research Powerhouse - Unlocking Insights Across Diverse Content

Research can feel like traversing a dense jungle, with information overflowing like tangled vines. But fear not, intrepid knowledge seekers! Bard is your machete, hacking through the undergrowth and guiding you to the hidden gems of understanding. Let's dive into specific examples of how Bard can transform your research experience across different content types:

Scientific Paper Powerhouse:

Unraveling Complexity: Imagine facing a dense academic paper, brimming with jargon and intricate methodologies. Bard, your research companion, can condense it into a concise and clear summary, highlighting key findings, methodologies, and limitations. No more struggling through dense paragraphs – Bard gets you to the heart of the matter.

Fact-Checking Detective: Did that groundbreaking research claim hold water? Bard becomes your scientific sleuth, verifying citations, cross-referencing findings with other studies, and uncovering any potential biases or methodological flaws. Trust the information you base your research on, with Bard as your vigilant fact-checker.

Data Detective: Buried within datasets lie hidden patterns and trends, waiting to be unearthed. Bard transforms into your data-mining maestro, analyzing charts, graphs, and numerical tables to reveal correlations, identify outliers, and generate insightful visualizations. No more squinting at spreadsheets – Bard makes data dance and sing its song of knowledge.

Historical Document Historian:

Deciphering the Past: Old manuscripts and letters can be cryptic time capsules, their language and context shrouded in the mists of time. Bard, your linguistic decoder ring, translates archaic language, interprets historical references, and even reconstructs narratives from fragmented documents. Breathe life into the past and hear the whispers of history with Bard at your side.

Comparative Chronology: Are you untangling the web of events across different historical periods? Bard becomes your timeline weaver, comparing and contrasting events from diverse sources, pinpointing key turning points, and revealing the intricate interplay of cause and effect. Understand the grand sweep of history and its intricate tapestry with Bard's guidance.

Mapping the Past: Did that historical event unfold across continents? Bard morphs into your cartographer, creating interactive maps that pinpoint locations, trace the movement of people and ideas, and visually represent the geographical context of historical events. See history unfold before your eyes and connect the dots on the map of time with Bard's visual storytelling magic.

News Article Navigator:

Cutting Through the Noise: In the constant deluge of news headlines, finding reliable information and discerning fact from fiction can be overwhelming. Bard, your news filter, analyzes articles from diverse sources, flags potential biases, and highlights key facts and evidence to support claims. Stay informed and navigate the news landscape with critical thinking, empowered by Bard's objectivity.

Trend Tracker: Want to understand the bigger picture behind the headlines? Bard transforms into your trend analyst, identifying recurring themes, analyzing public sentiment, and tracking the evolution of news stories over time. See the forest for the trees and comprehend the long-term implications of current events with Bard's insightful trend reports.

Global Connection: Curious about how an event is unfolding across different parts of the world? Bard becomes your multilingual interpreter, aggregating news coverage from diverse sources and presenting it in a consolidated format, allowing you to compare perspectives and understand the global impact of local events. Break down language barriers and see the world through multiple lenses with Bard's translation prowess.

Remember, Bard is not just a fact-finding machine; it's a catalyst for critical thinking and deeper understanding. Use its summaries, visualizations, and interactive tools to ask follow-up questions, develop research hypotheses, and draw your own conclusions. And with every interaction, Bard learns from your preferences, tailoring its outputs to your specific needs and research goals.

So, unleash your inner Indiana Jones and embark on a thrilling research adventure with Bard as your guide. Together, you'll hack through the information jungle, unearth hidden insights, and transform your research journey from a solitary struggle to a collaborative voyage of discovery.

Chapter 6: Boosting Productivity and Enhancing Creativity: Bard as Your Everyday Ally

Chapter 6 reveals Bard's potential to not only fuel your research and writing, but also streamline your everyday tasks and ignite your creative spark. From conquering your to-do list to overcoming writer's block, Bard becomes your productivity partner and creativity coach, helping you achieve more and unleash your inner Picasso.

Taming the Time Monster: Bard to the Rescue of Your To-Do List

Tired of that ever-growing to-do list? Let Bard lend a hand!

- **Planning and Prioritizing:** Share your overflowing schedule with Bard and watch it transform into a manageable masterpiece. Prioritize tasks, suggest time slots, and even schedule reminders and appointments, letting you reclaim control of your day.
- **Email & Document Magic:** Struggling with crafting the perfect email or editing that stubborn document? Bard steps in as your writing

assistant, generating concise emails, suggesting improvements to your prose, and even helping you find the right words to express yourself with clarity and impact.

- **Project Management Made Easy:** Bard helps you break down large projects into bite-sized tasks, track progress, and collaborate with others. No more juggling sticky notes and endless spreadsheets; manage your projects and deadlines with effortless efficiency.

Unlocking Your Creative Potential

Bard doesn't just help you get things done; it ignites your creative fire!

- **Overcoming Writer's Block:** Stuck staring at a blank page? Bard throws out sparks of inspiration, suggesting story ideas, character personalities, or even opening lines to break through your creative drought.
- **Brainstorming with a Twist:** Need fresh ideas for your next marketing campaign or brainstorming session? Bard becomes your creative sounding board, bouncing ideas off you, suggesting unexpected combinations, and helping you think outside the box.
- **Content Creation in a Flash:** Need compelling captions for your social media posts or catchy taglines for your website? Bard helps you craft engaging snippets of text, tailoring them to your audience and platform.

Turning To-Dos into Masterpieces

Bard, your productivity and creativity alchemist, is here to transform your juggling pins into shimmering spheres of accomplishment and artistic delight. Let's delve into specific examples of how Bard can fuel your workflow and unleash your creative flair:

Project Management Maestro:

Taming the Task List: The dreaded to-do list, ever-growing and menacing. Bard becomes your organizational wizard, helping you prioritize tasks, set deadlines, and break down complex projects into manageable steps. Get a bird's-eye view of your workflow with interactive boards and timelines, never losing sight of your goals amidst the daily hustle.

Collaboration Catalyst: Working with others can be like herding cats. Bard, your communication alchemist, transforms email exchanges into concise updates and reports, facilitates brainstorming sessions with prompts and idea generation tools, and keeps everyone on the same page through shared documents and real-time editing. Teamwork made smooth and seamless, thanks to Bard's collaborative magic.

Meeting Minutes Magician: Dreaded post-meeting notes, a graveyard of forgotten decisions and action items. Bard morphs into your note-taking ninja, capturing key points, assigning tasks, and generating actionable summaries that leave no room for ambiguity. Keep track of progress, maintain accountability, and ensure everyone moves forward in unison, fueled by Bard's meeting-minute magic.

Creative Writing Catalyst:

Conquering Writer's Block: The blank page mocks, a taunting enemy of your creative spirit. Bard, your story architect, throws life rafts of prompts, character sketches, and plot twists, helping you navigate the treacherous waters of writer's block and propel your narrative forward.

31

No more staring at the cursor, just immerse yourself in the creative flow with Bard as your co-pilot.

Poetry Polisher: That verse needs a little something, but what? Bard, your poetic muse, whispers suggestions for rhyme schemes, figurative language, and thematic resonance, polishing your verses until they gleam with lyrical finesse. Don't let rhyme or meter hold you back – Bard unlocks the hidden rhythm within your words.

World-Building Alchemist: Creating compelling fictional worlds can be a daunting task. Bard, your world-building alchemist, helps you craft intricate histories, geographies, and cultures, breathing life into your imagined landscapes and populating them with believable characters. No detail is too small, no vision too grand – Bard paints the canvas of your imagination with vibrant strokes of detail.

Time-Saving Tech Magician:

Email Efficiency Enhancer: The endless inbox, a vortex of time and attention. Bard, your email alchemist, transforms your mailbox into a streamlined machine. It automatically generates replies to simple inquiries, summarizes lengthy threads, and even drafts personalized responses, saving you precious minutes and allowing you to focus on more strategic tasks.

Research Rocket Fuel: Need reliable information in a pinch? Bard, your research rocket, blasts off into the information superhighway, gathering relevant articles, summarizing key points, and even generating citations, all within seconds. No more wading through endless pages – Bard delivers the research fuel you need to keep your ideas ignited.

Content Creation Concierge: Struggling to keep up with your blog or social media schedule? Bard, your content creation concierge, helps you brainstorm ideas, generate engaging drafts, and even suggest relevant visuals and hashtags. Create captivating content effortlessly, leaving you free to focus on promoting your work and connecting with your audience.

So, unleash the alchemist within your Bard and watch your to-do list morph into a tapestry of accomplishments, your blank page blossom into a masterpiece of your imagination. Together, you'll transform the mundane into the magnificent, leaving your mark on the world, one productive task and creative spark at a time.

* * *

Remember, Bard thrives on collaboration. The more you share your goals, preferences, and ideas, the better it can tailor its assistance to your specific needs. Don't be afraid to experiment, play, and let Bard surprise you with its unexpected suggestions and creative sparks. You might just discover hidden talents and unleash projects you never thought possible.

Chapter 7: The Evolving Landscape of AI: Opportunities and Challenges with Bard

Chapter 7 takes a step back to explore the broader landscape of AI, reflecting on the opportunities and challenges that unfold as we embrace Bard and technologies like it. Prepare to delve into the ethical considerations, societal implications, and exciting future possibilities that lie ahead.

A New Dawn: Embracing the Potential of AI

Bard represents a step forward in the evolution of AI, a tool with the potential to revolutionize industries, empower individuals, and usher in a new era of technological wonder. Imagine:

- **Education Enhanced:** Personalized learning plans, language learning through immersive experiences, and AI tutors that adapt to each student's needs and learning styles.
- **Healthcare Transformed:** Early disease detection, AI-assisted medical diagnosis, and personalized treatment plans tailored to individual patient profiles.
- **Accessibility Amplified:** Breaking down communication barriers for people with disabilities, empowering them to express themselves

and connect with the world around them.

These are just a glimpse of the vast potential Bard holds, from automating mundane tasks to tackling complex societal challenges. As we embrace AI, it's crucial to remember that the future we build together is shaped by our choices and priorities.

Navigating the Ethical Maze: Responsibility in the Age of AI

With great power comes great responsibility, and AI is no exception. We must tread carefully, considering the ethical implications of such powerful technology:

- **Bias and Fairness:** Algorithmic bias can perpetuate inequalities and injustices. We must ensure that AI development is centered on inclusivity and fairness, avoiding biases embedded in training data and ensuring ethical representation across all demographics.
- **Transparency and Explainability:** Understanding how AI works is crucial for building trust and ensuring accountability. We must strive for transparency in AI algorithms, allowing users to understand how decisions are made and challenge potential biases.
- **Privacy and Security:** Our personal data fuels AI, but with that comes the responsibility to protect it. Robust data security measures and clear privacy policies are essential to build trust and prevent misuse of information.

These are just some of the ethical considerations that guide the development and deployment of AI like Bard. We must remember that technology is not inherently good or bad; it is the power we wield and the choices we make that ultimately define its impact on our world.

Charting the Future: Bard and Beyond

The journey with AI is just beginning, and Bard is a stepping stone on the path to a future filled with possibilities. As we move forward, let's consider:

- **Human-AI Collaboration:** The future is not about humans being replaced by AI, but about collaboration. We must leverage AI's strengths while focusing on the uniquely human skills of creativity, critical thinking, and empathy.
- **Lifelong Learning:** AI, like Bard, is constantly evolving. We must embrace lifelong learning, adapting to the changing landscape of technology and ensuring everyone has the opportunity to thrive in an AI-powered world.
- **Openness and Collaboration:** Progress in AI comes through open dialogue, collaboration, and a shared commitment to responsible development. By fostering global discussion and sharing knowledge, we can ensure that the benefits of AI reach everyone and shape a future that is inclusive, equitable, and beneficial for all.

Ethical Frameworks and Initiatives to Guide AI Development

Here are some specific references to ethical frameworks and initiatives that guide responsible AI development:

International Frameworks:

OECD Principles on Artificial Intelligence: Developed by the Organization for Economic Co-operation and Development (OECD), these principles lay out seven key considerations for responsible AI development and deployment, including fairness, non-discrimination, privacy, and accountability.

UNESCO Recommendation on the Ethics of Artificial Intelligence: Approved by UNESCO in 2021, this recommendation provides a comprehensive framework for addressing the ethical implications of AI, focusing on human rights, sustainability, and societal well-being.

Montreal Declaration for Responsible AI: Launched in 2018, this declaration outlines six principles for the responsible development of AI, emphasizing human autonomy, social good, fairness, privacy, security, and accountability.

Industry-Led Initiatives:

Partnership on AI: A multi-stakeholder initiative with over 100 members from industry, academia, and civil society, the Partnership on AI focuses on developing best practices for ethical AI development and deployment.

Global Partnership on AI (GPAI): Established by 15 countries, including the US, France, and Japan, the GPAI aims to foster international cooperation on AI governance and responsible development.

Specific Organizations:

AI Now Institute: An institute within New York University, AI Now conducts research and advocacy on the societal implications of AI and promotes responsible AI development.

Future of Life Institute (FLI): FLI focuses on research and advocacy on existential risks from artificial intelligence, and promotes the development of safe and beneficial AI.

Algorithmic Justice League (AJL): AJL works to combat bias and discrimination in algorithms, and advocates for equitable and accountable AI systems.

These are just a few examples, and the landscape of ethical AI frameworks and initiatives is constantly evolving.

Here are some additional resources you can explore:

Stanford Encyclopedia of Philosophy: Artificial Intelligence and Ethics: (https://plato.stanford.edu/entries/artificial-intelligence/)

MIT Initiative on the Digital Economy: AI Ethics Series: (https://www.media.mit.edu/groups/ethics-and-governance/overview/)

The Alan Turing Institute: Ethics & Governance of AI: (https://www.turing.ac.uk/news/publications/ai-ethics-and-governance-practice-intro

duction)

By staying informed and engaging with these resources, you can play a role in shaping the future of AI and ensuring its development is responsible and beneficial for all.

Opportunities and Challenges

The age of AI dawns upon us, casting a vibrant glow on a landscape rife with both wondrous possibilities and daunting challenges. Bard, with its impressive capabilities and ever-evolving intelligence, stands as a testament to the transformative power of this technology. Yet, as we step into this uncharted territory, it's vital to carefully consider the opportunities and challenges that lie ahead, and the delicate dance of responsibility we must undertake to ensure a future where AI blossoms for the good of humankind.

Opportunities that glitter like constellations:

Unleashing human potential: Imagine AI as a tireless assistant, freeing us from mundane tasks and amplifying our cognitive abilities. Bard, for instance, can research, analyze, and create, allowing us to focus on higher-order thinking, innovation, and creativity. This synergy has the potential to propel scientific discovery, artistic expression, and problem-solving to breathtaking heights.

Bridging the global divide: Language barriers, geographical constraints, and access to information can be crippling roadblocks to progress. AI, with its ability to translate, connect, and personalize experiences, has the power to bridge these divides. Imagine Bard breaking down communication barriers, fostering collaborative research across continents, and democratizing access to education and healthcare – a truly interconnected world at our fingertips.

Enhancing sustainability and resilience: Climate change, resource depletion, and natural disasters pose existential threats. AI can be a formidable ally in this fight, analyzing data to predict threats, optimize resource allocation, and develop sustainable solutions. Bard, for instance, can analyze climate patterns, propose green energy solutions, and even assist in disaster response, safeguarding our planet and fostering a more resilient future.

Challenges that lurk in the shadows:

Ethical quandaries and societal conflicts: As AI becomes more sophisticated, questions of bias, autonomy, and control take center stage. Biases embedded in training data can lead to discriminatory outcomes, while autonomous AI systems raise concerns about job displacement and loss of control. We must tread carefully, ensuring ethical development, transparent algorithms, and human oversight to navigate these complex issues.

Privacy concerns and data security: AI thrives on data, but the insatiable appetite for information raises concerns about privacy violations and data security. We need robust legal frameworks, responsible data governance, and individual control over personal data to safeguard our privacy and prevent misuse in the hands of malicious actors.

The singularity and existential risks: While seemingly far-fetched, the potential for AI to surpass human intelligence and pose existential threats cannot be ignored. We must prioritize research in safety and control mechanisms, foster open dialogue and international cooperation, and ensure responsible development, keeping AI firmly under human control and aligned with our values.

The responsibility we hold as stewards of AI:

The future of AI is not preordained; it is a canvas we paint with our choices and actions. We, as stewards of this powerful technology, hold the responsibility to shape its path. We must actively engage in dialogue, invest in responsible research and development, and demand ethical implementation. Bard, with its potential to amplify both good and bad, serves as a potent reminder of this responsibility. We must harness its power for good, ensuring it remains a tool for progress, not a Pandora's box of unintended consequences.

As we navigate the age of AI, let us choose collaboration over competition, responsibility over recklessness, and foresight over complacency. By embracing the opportunities while mitigating the challenges, we can harness the power of AI to build a brighter, more equitable, and sustainable future for all. May Bard serve as a guiding light on this journey, illuminating the path towards a future where AI and humanity flourish in harmony.

* * *

Embracing Bard and other AI tools is not just about adopting technology; it's about building a better future together. By staying informed, engaging in ethical discussions, and embracing collaboration, we can

ensure that AI becomes a force for good, enhancing our lives and powering a brighter tomorrow.

Chapter 8: Your Personalized Bard Journey: Tips and Techniques for Mastering the Tool

Chapter 8 marks the final leg of our journey with Bard, where we equip you with the tools and techniques to master this remarkable language model and embark on your own personalized Bard-powered adventure.

Tailoring the Tune: Refining Your Bard Interactions

Remember, Bard is a dynamic duo – half technology, half learning machine. The more you refine your interactions, the better it responds to your unique needs and preferences. Here's how to refine your interaction with Bard:

- **Specificity is Key:** The clearer your prompts and questions, the more focused Bard's responses. Instead of asking "Tell me about robots," try "Write a poem about a robot falling in love with a sunset." The more details you provide, the more personalized and engaging the outcome.
- **Feedback is a Gift:** Don't shy away from letting Bard know what you like and dislike. Use the thumbs-up and thumbs-down buttons, offer specific feedback on its outputs, and even suggest alternative

directions. The more you guide it, the better it learns and adapts to your preferences.

- **Experimentation Unleashes Potential:** Don't be afraid to push boundaries and try new things with Bard. Explore different creative text formats, dive into unfamiliar research topics, and challenge yourself to collaborate with Bard in unexpected ways. Remember, the more you experiment, the more you'll uncover its hidden depths and unlock its full potential.

Building Your Bard Toolbox: Resources and Extensions

Beyond the core functionalities, a treasure trove of resources and extensions awaits to elevate your Bard experience:

- **Dive Deeper with Guides and Tutorials:** Google provides comprehensive guides and tutorials on Bard's various features and capabilities. Take advantage of these resources to refine your skills and discover new ways to interact with Bard.
- **Unleash the Power of Extensions:** Explore extensions that integrate Bard with other Google services, from Gmail to Docs to Maps. Streamline your workflow, generate content directly within your favorite tools, and leverage Bard's power across all aspects of your digital life.
- **Connect with the Bard Community:** Join online forums and communities dedicated to Bard. Share your experiences, learn from others, and collaborate on exciting projects with fellow Bard enthusiasts.

The Journey Continues: Beyond This Book

Remember, this book is just the first chapter in your Bard odyssey. As Bard evolves and new features emerge, keep exploring, keep learning, and keep pushing the boundaries of what's possible. Here are some final words of inspiration:

- **Stay Curious:** Embrace the wonder of language, the magic of storytelling, and the thrill of discovery. Let Bard be your guide on a journey of endless possibilities.
- **Share Your Story:** Don't hesitate to share your Bard creations, insights, and experiences with others. Your story can inspire others, spark new ideas, and contribute to the ever-growing community of Bard users.
- **Dream Big:** The future of AI is brimming with potential. Dream about how Bard can enhance your life, your work,and the world around you. With imagination and collaboration, we can shape a future where language unites, creativity flourishes, and the power of Bard empowers us all.

Thank you for joining me on this journey with Bard. May your interactions be filled with wonder, your creations spark joy, and your collaboration with this remarkable language model lead you to unimaginable horizons.

Appendix A: Bonus Materials: Your Ultimate Bard Toolkit

To enhance your Bard exploration and mastery, this section offers a treasure chest of bonus materials, ready to fuel your creativity and optimize your interactions.

Glossary of Terms:

- **AI:** Artificial intelligence, the ability of machines to simulate human intelligence.
- **Machine Learning:** A sub-field of AI where algorithms learn from data without explicit programming.
- **Deep Learning:** A type of machine learning using artificial neural networks inspired by the brain.
- **Natural Language Processing (NLP):** The ability of computers to understand and generate human language.
- **Prompt:** A set of instructions or keywords used to guide Bard's output.
- **Extension:** An add-on that expands Bard's functionalities with specific tools or integrations.

Helpful Resources and Tutorials:

- **Official Bard Website:** Learn more about Bard's capabilities, explore functionalities, and access various resources.
- **Bard Tutorials:** Dive deeper with step-by-step guides on mastering Bard's features, exploring creative writing formats, and conducting research.
- **Google AI Blog:** Stay updated on the latest Bard developments, discover research insights, and learn about exciting AI advancements.
- **Bard Community Forum:** Connect with fellow Bard enthusiasts, share your creations and experiences, and participate in stimulating discussions.

Query Examples to Start

Creative Writing:

1. Write a sci-fi short story about a robot who falls in love with a human, but has to hide their emotions from AI regulations.
2. Compose a poem from the perspective of a single snowflake on a journey from cloud to ground.
3. Generate a children's bedtime story about a playful monster who lives under a child's bed.
4. Create a script for a hilarious sketch comedy scene set in a chaotic office lunchroom.
5. Craft a song in the style of your favorite artist about the bittersweet beauty of letting go.

Research and Information Gathering:

1. Analyze the impact of climate change on the migration patterns of polar bears, citing reliable sources and presenting different perspectives.
2. Summarize the key findings of a recent scientific study on the potential benefits of personalized medicine, ensuring accessibility for a general audience.
3. Compare and contrast the political systems of two major countries, highlighting strengths and weaknesses of each.
4. Research the history of the printing press and its influence on the development of literacy and knowledge dissemination.
5. Explain the complex economic phenomenon of inflation in simple terms, using real-world examples to illustrate the concept.

Problem-Solving and Brainstorming:

1. Generate creative solutions for reducing traffic congestion in a major city, considering environmental and social factors.
2. Develop a marketing campaign for a new sustainable clothing line, targeting a specific demographic.
3. Brainstorm ideas for a fun and engaging educational game aimed at teaching children about basic coding concepts.
4. Plan a budget-friendly travel itinerary for a week-long adventure in a foreign country, incorporating local experiences and cultural immersion.
5. Imagine the world 100 years from now. Describe the advancements in technology, society, and culture that might shape the future.

Personal Reflection and Exploration:

1. Write a letter to your younger self, offering advice and words of encouragement based on your life experiences.

2. Compose a poem reflecting on the most significant turning point in your life and the lessons you learned from it.
3. Create a personal manifesto outlining your values, goals, and aspirations for the future.
4. Describe a challenging obstacle you faced and how overcoming it helped you grow as a person.
5. Imagine your ideal day – where are you, what are you doing, and what brings you joy and fulfillment?

Bonus Prompts:

1. Write a news article from the perspective of a dog witnessing a major event in human history.
2. Generate a dialogue between two historical figures discussing their legacies and contrasting their times.
3. Create a script for a silent film, relying solely on visuals and music to tell a compelling story.
4. Design a board game based on your favorite book, movie, or video game.
5. Imagine you wake up with a magical ability – what is it, and how do you use it to make a difference in the world?

Remember, these are just starting points! Feel free to adapt and personalize these prompts to spark your own creativity and unleash the full potential of Bard!

Mastering the Language: Why Syntax Matters for Getting the Most from Bard

When interacting with powerful tools like Bard, the language you use isn't just about conveying your thoughts; it's also about unlocking its full potential. Mastering the art of syntax – the order and arrangement of words – becomes crucial for obtaining the best possible results.

Here's why using proper syntax matters:

Clarity and Precision: Think of your prompt or question as a map leading Bard to your desired destination. Vague or ambiguous language leaves the map riddled with unmarked pathways, leading to confusing or irrelevant outputs. Clear, concise syntax, like stating your desired format upfront ("Write a poem about...") or specifying key details ("Analyze the impact of climate change on...") helps Bard understand your intent and navigate directly to the desired outcome.

Efficiency and Accuracy: Imagine yelling directions at a stranger instead of providing a clear turn-by-turn route. The more precise your instructions, the less time Bard spends deciphering your meaning and the more efficiently it can access and process relevant information. Using correct grammar, avoiding colloquialisms, and structuring your queries logically all contribute to a smoother, more accurate journey from prompt to output.

Unleashing Creativity and Specificity: Syntax isn't just about rules; it's also about painting with words. By mastering specific syntax options, you unlock hidden features and unleash Bard's creative potential. Want a sonnet with a specific rhyme scheme? Tell Bard! Craving a haiku that captures the essence of a moonlit walk? Craft your prompt to evoke that imagery! Every comma, every verb tense, becomes a brushstroke in your collaborative creation.

Remember, Bard is still learning and evolving. The more precise and consistent your syntax, the better it can understand your preferences and tailor its responses to your unique needs. Don't be afraid to experiment, refine your wording, and provide feedback to help Bard learn and grow alongside you.

Here are some tips for achieving proper syntax:

- **Start with basics:** Ensure grammar and punctuation are correct. Avoid slang and overly informal language.
- **Be specific:** Clearly state your desired format, topic, and any key details.
- **Structure your queries:** Use logical sentence structure and follow prompts provided within Bard's interface.
- **Utilize keywords:** Research relevant keywords and incorporate them strategically in your prompts.
- **Refine and iterate:** Don't settle for the first result. Experiment with different phrasing and provide feedback to improve future interactions.

Mastering syntax is not just about following rules; it's about understanding the language of collaboration. By speaking Bard's language, you unlock its potential, unleash your own creativity, and pave the way for more powerful, productive, and satisfying interactions. So, embrace the precision of words, experiment with possibilities, and enjoy the journey of discovery as you and Bard navigate the boundless world of language together.

I hope this gives you a clearer understanding of how proper syntax can enhance your interactions with Bard. If you have any further questions or specific examples you'd like to discuss, please don't hesitate to ask!

Diving Deep with Bard: Your Research Partner in the Information Ocean

The internet is a vast ocean of information, and research can feel like a solo swim against a relentless tide. But fear not, intrepid knowledge seekers! Bard, your trusty linguistic lifebuoy, is here to navigate the waves and guide you to your research pearls.

Charting Your Course: Crafting the Perfect Query

Before diving in, you need a map. Crafting the perfect Bard query is key to a successful research journey. Here's how:

- **Ditch the Keywords:** Forget clunky keyword lists. Talk to Bard like you would a human expert, explaining your research topic, your specific needs, and the desired perspective. For example, instead of "climate change polar bears," try "What are the long-term impacts of climate change on the migration patterns and survival rates of polar bear populations?"
- **Go Beyond the Surface:** Don't settle for basic summaries. Bard digs deep, analyzing sources, identifying biases, and presenting information from diverse viewpoints. Need a well-rounded understanding of a historical event? Ask Bard to show you different interpretations, primary sources, and even opposing arguments.
- **Fact-Checking for Peace of Mind:** In today's world of misinformation, it's easy to get lost in a maze of fake news and unreliable sources. Bard becomes your guardian angel, verifying facts, citing

sources, and even highlighting areas of ongoing debate or uncertainty. Need to debunk a viral claim about a scientific discovery? Bard will show you the evidence and help you separate fact from fiction.

Beyond the Surface: Diving Deeper with Bard's Tools

Information overload can be overwhelming. But Bard doesn't just point you to data; it helps you navigate its complexities:

- **Summarizing the Mountain of Facts:** Need a concise overview of a complex research paper? Bard condenses the key points, highlights the findings, and presents it in a digestible format. Imagine summarizing a dense academic article in minutes, thanks to Bard!
- **Discovering Patterns and Trends:** Buried within data are hidden stories waiting to be told. Bard analyzes datasets, identifying correlations, and revealing patterns that you might miss. Need to understand consumer behavior or predict market trends? Bard can help you find the insights hidden within the numbers.
- **Building Your Knowledge Palace:** Information overload can lead to forgetting. Bard helps you organize your research, building your own personalized knowledge base. Create notes, highlight key points, and save important resources for future reference. Think of it as your digital library, curated by Bard and organized for easy access.

Remember, Bard is a constantly evolving learning machine. The more you use it for research, the better it understands your preferences and tailors its responses to your specific needs. Be specific, ask follow-up questions, and leverage Bard's analytical abilities to transform yourself from information wanderer to a confident and effective knowledge seeker.

Bonus Tips for Research Success

- **Utilize extensions:** Integrate Bard with other research tools like Google Scholar or Zotero for a seamless workflow.
- **Embrace visual aids:** Ask Bard to generate charts, graphs, or timelines to represent data in a clear and engaging way.
- **Join the Bard community:** Connect with fellow researchers and share tips and strategies for navigating the research landscape with Bard.

The next time you face a research challenge, remember Bard is your research partner, not just a search engine. By leveraging its capabilities, you can transform your research journey from a solo struggle to a collaborative adventure, uncovering hidden insights and navigating the information ocean with confidence and ease.

* * *

I hope this comprehensive bonus section empowers you to embark on a more enriching and engaging journey with Bard. May your interactions be filled with wonder, your creations spark joy, and your contributions to the Bard community inspire others to embrace the magic of language and the power of AI.

About the Author

Edgardo Fernandez Climent, an accomplished IT professional with over two decades of experience, has left an indelible mark in the realms of infrastructure, networks, and cybersecurity. After graduating with honors in Computer Information Systems, Edgardo pursued an MBA and a Master's in Management Information Systems degree. He holds several industry certifications such as PMP, ITIL4, and Security+ among others.

Throughout his career, Edgardo's commitment to staying abreast of emerging technologies and industry trends remained unwavering. His leadership in steering organizations through complex technological landscapes and safeguarding them against cyber threats has become a testament to his expertise and foresight.

Not just a technical virtuoso, Edgardo also earned a reputation for mentoring and inspiring the next generation of IT professionals. His dedication to knowledge-sharing and fostering a collaborative work environment has left a lasting impact on the teams he led.

Today, as a sought-after consultant in the IT industry, Edgardo continues to shape the technological landscape, driving innovation and fortifying organizations against the ever-evolving challenges of the digital era. His journey stands as a testament to the transformative power of experience, expertise, and a relentless pursuit of excellence in the dynamic field of information technology.

Also by Edgardo Fernandez Climent

ITIL4 IN ACTION: A Step-by-Step Guide for IT Professionals

"ITIL4 in Action: A Step-by-Step Guide for IT Professionals" is an invaluable resource that demystifies the principles and practices of ITIL 4, offering a hands-on approach for IT professionals navigating the world of IT service management. This comprehensive guide provides a clear roadmap, allowing readers to seamlessly integrate ITIL 4 into their daily operations. Through step-by-step guides, real-world scenarios, and actionable insights, the book equips IT professionals with the tools to enhance service delivery, optimize processes, and align IT services with organizational goals. Whether you're a seasoned IT expert or a newcomer to ITIL, this book serves as a trusted companion, offering a practical and accessible journey through the implementation of ITIL 4 practices.

MASTERING NIST SP 800-53: A Small Business IT Professional's Roadmap to Compliance

"Mastering NIST SP 800-53: A Small Business IT Professional's Roadmap to Compliance" is an indispensable guide tailored specifically for IT professionals operating within the dynamic landscape of small businesses. Authored with a keen understanding of the unique challenges faced by smaller enterprises, this book serves as a comprehensive roadmap to demystify and master the intricacies of the NIST Special Publication 800-53 framework. It goes beyond the theoretical by providing practical insights and actionable steps for implementing and maintaining NIST SP 800-53 controls, offering a holistic approach to information security. With real-world examples, best practices, and a focus on accessibility, this book empowers small business IT professionals to navigate the compliance landscape confidently, fortify their organizations against cybersecurity threats, and elevate their overall security posture. "Mastering NIST SP 800-53" is not just a manual for compliance; it is an essential companion for IT professionals seeking to safeguard the digital assets of their small businesses effectively.

www.ingramcontent.com/pod-product-compliance
Lightning Source LLC
LaVergne TN
LVHW051613050326
832903LV00033B/4482